This collection is particularly close to my heart.

Firstly, as a chef, I am proud to support my colleagues, who are among the best in the world, in this adventure of the transmission of their knowledge to as many people as possible. It is important for me to organize an international community of talented artisans of flavor, we have so much to share with the public!

Secondly, as a publisher, I decided to create this collection in order to offer the best recipes by the best chefs in the world in an accessible format. I came up with it out of my desire to transfer quality content and originality. I did not want the educational aspect of the step-by-step presentation, in which lies the true value of these books, to spoil the beauty of the object.

Eric's achievement is exemplary and shows that the ability to adapt is critical to a chef's success! His greatest quality is this ability to evolve his cuisine and performance without ever compromising excellence. For more than twenty years since his debut at Le Bernardin, he has been offering and improving upon seafood cuisine of the highest order, and he has been able to make the most of New York's cultural riches. He draws inspiration from all the corners of the world, from cultures as disparate as Peru, Vietnam, and Brazil. This is what makes Eric a great chef: his interest in listening to others and broadening his own horizons, whether it be in culinary or human heritage!

— Alain Ducasse

my BEST ERIC RIPERT

ALAIN DUCASSE
PUBLISHING

ERIC RIPERT

What chefs have taught you the most?

When I left culinary school I knew I needed to learn a more contemporary approach to cooking. I wanted to learn at a Michelin—rated restaurant. I was lucky to end up with a position at La Tour d'Argent. That was a key position for me because I knew that I needed to start out in a serious restaurant.

From there, I went to work for Joël Robuchon and it was there, under his tutelage, that I really learned how to be a technician. I learned the disciplines and techniques of a good line cook. But I was ready for more. It was Robuchon who encouraged me to move to the United States and connected me with Jean-Louis Palladin. Working in Paris under Robuchon was like playing an instrument in a classical orchestra—cooking in Palladin's kitchen was like going from the orchestra to Woodstock. My mind was opened under Jean-Louis' influence. He taught me to be creative and have no fear.

After working at the Watergate Hotel with Chef Palladin I ended up in New York. It was essential to me to move to New York because it is a city that never stops changing—there is always the challenge to keep exploring. I began working at Le Bernardin in 1991 under chef and owner Gilbert LeCoze. It was there that I learned how to be a leader. I had learned the stages of a classic kitchen; I had labored to understand the timing and technique of working a busy line in Michelin—starred restaurants. I learned to push fear aside and be imaginative with my creations. Gilbert was the mentor who saw that I was ready to lead the kitchen and be an executive chef.

Was the transition at Le Bernardin, from being chef de cuisine to suddenly executive chef, difficult?

Losing Gilbert suddenly in 1994 was very sad and psychologically a great loss, but I was ready to take on the challenge of running the kitchen at Le Bernardin. He had been training me to take on more and more responsibility and giving me a lot of creative freedom, so technically and creatively, I was comfortable.

How have you evolved as a leader in your kitchen at Le Bernardin?

The collaborative process has become very important in our kitchen. Being the mentor to a team means that you have to show them and let them understand your process but allow them to be a part of the creative collaboration. I like the dynamic because it's interactive and we can work together to make the best menu possible.

The order and structure within the kitchen at Le Bernardin is impressive and without drama. How are you able to maintain that environment?

I used to run the kitchen with more of an iron fist but several years back I decided that wasn't the best way to operate and began to change. Being an abusive chef does not get good results in the long run. We operate on a policy of mutual respect for each other and getting the job done correctly together. The organization of the kitchen allows everyone to work without too much stress, and while we do operate on a brigade – style structure, each position is highly valued. We get better results and in the end everyone, including the customer, is happy.

FIVE KEY DATES *1982*
|
Graduated culinary school and went to work at La Tour d'Argent in Paris at age seventeen.

1989
|
Moved to Washington, D.C. to work with Jean-Louis Palladin at the Watergate Hotel.

1991
|
Moved to New York and started working at Le Bernardin.

What do you believe is the reason Le Bernardin has maintained such high critical acclaim consistently for many years?

Most of it has to do with our standards of operation within the entire company—front of the house, back of the house, in the office, everywhere. Moreover, being in New York is energizing and the city itself encourages you to be at your best. You have to evolve and change with what is happening around you or you will stop. There is talent coming in from all over the planet all the time, and there are always new restaurants opening and good things happening. It's challenging, and I think that the competition is good—it keeps you on your toes.

How do you define your culinary style?

My approach to the creation of a dish at Le Bernardin is to first and foremost make the fish the star of the plate. No matter what other elements go with a particular dish, the fish will always be in the spotlight—the other ingredients must elevate the fish. I also believe that you have to stay open—minded in order to keep moving forward. Lots of inspiration comes from my travels, and it's important to me to keep exploring new styles and cultures. Exposure to what other people are doing, whether it is here at home or on the other side of the globe, keeps me curious and excited to do more. Those influences always find their way onto the plate.

How have you managed to organize the layers of responsibility you have between your restaurant, charity work, successful television and book efforts, and family?

I have committed to dividing my journey into three parts: Family / Business / Myself

Being realistic about my schedule and keeping these three facets of my life in balance is crucial. Understanding my responsibilities and priorities is one of the reasons that I haven't opened other restaurants. I'm content and don't need more than what I have now.

CULINARY **SNAPSHOT**

1/ WHAT UTENSIL CAN YOU NOT BE WITHOUT?
A good knife.

2/ WHAT IS YOUR FAVORITE DRINK?
There are three: tequila, Bordeaux, and Scotch.

3/ DO YOU EVER USE COOKBOOKS?
I use cookbooks for the visual inspiration—I love the photos.

4/ WHAT IS YOUR CULINARY INDULGENCE?
Dark chocolate.

5/ IF YOU HADN'T BECOME A CHEF, WHAT WOULD YOU BE?
A forest ranger.

6/ WHAT DO YOU COLLECT?
Buddha statues, but that is a weakness because you are not supposed to be attached.

7/ WHAT DO YOU COOK AT HOME?
Seasonal, fresh, and organic food—always.

8/ WHAT IS YOUR MOTTO?
Be yourself.

1995

At the age of twenty-nine, Chef Ripert received the third New York Times four stars review for Le Bernardin. The restaurant has since received four stars in 2005 and 2012.

2005

Le Bernardin receives three Michelin Stars in the first year of their New York guide, and has maintained three stars every year since—nine years in a row.

TABLE OF CON TENTS

RED SNAPPER
AND CEPES IN PORT REDUCTION

44

SALMON
RED WINE BÉARNAISE

52

SEA
MEDLEY

60

SHRIMP, TOMATO,
AND BASIL "PIZZA"

70

SMOKED SALMON
CROQUE MONSIEUR WITH CAVIAR

78

LOBSTER
CAPUCCINO

86

FLUKE

This dish is inspired by my travels to Peru.
The ceviches start with a simple base recipe,
then, with the addition of a few ingredients,
increase in complexity and intensity.

RECIPE

FLUKE

- ☐ 8 ounces (225 g) sushi-quality fluke fillet
- ☐ Fine sea salt
- ☐ Freshly ground white pepper
- ☐ Espelette pepper

FLUKE JUICE

- ☐ 6 ounces (170 g) fluke fillet, diced
- ☐ ¾ cups (180 ml) lemon juice
- ☐ ¾ cups (180 ml) fresh lime juice
- ☐ 1 tablespoon sugar

- ☐ 1 tablespoon fine sea salt
- ☐ ½ small red onion, peeled and sliced

FIRST MARINADE

- ☐ 6 tablespoons (80 ml) fluke juice
- ☐ 2 tablespoons cilantro, julienned
- ☐ 2 tablespoons red onion, julienned
- ☐ 1 teaspoon pique

SECOND MARINADE

- ☐ 6 tablespoons (80 ml) fluke juice

- ☐ 2 tablespoons fresh cilantro, julienned
- ☐ 2 tablespoons red onion, julienned
- ☐ 1 teaspoon pique
- ☐ 1 tablespoon tomato, brunoised
- ☐ 1 teaspoon jalapeno, minced
- ☐ 2 teaspoons mint, julienned
- ☐ 2 teaspoons basil, julienned
- ☐ 4 teaspoons extra-virgin olive oil

THIRD MARINADE

- ☐ 4 tablespoons (60 ml) fluke juice

- ☐ ¾ teaspoon pique
- ☐ ¾ tablespoon tomato, brunoised
- ☐ 1 tablespoon ponzu
- ☐ ⅜ teaspoon wasabi paste
- ☐ ¾ teaspoon ginger oil
- ☐ 1 ½ teaspoons scallion, thinly sliced
- ☐ ¾ teaspoon orange zest, finely grated
- ☐ 1 ½ tablespoons soy sauce

FINISHING

- ☐ Espelette pepper
- ☐ Curry powder

Fluke

Slice the fluke fillet, on the bias, into ½-by-2-inch (12-by-5-cm) slivers. You will need about 16 slices for each portion. Lay the slivers flat on a large plate. Cover the plate with plastic wrap and keep refrigerated.

01

Fluke juice

Combine all of the ingredients in a small bowl. Cover and let marinate refrigerated for 1 hour. Strain through a fine-mesh sieve. Reserve.

02

Marinades

Prepare each of the marinades by combining all of the ingredients for each marinade in three separate bowls. Prepare the first marinade.

Prepare the second marinade.

After the fluke is placed in the marinade, you must work quickly to plate and serve, as the acid will start to cook the fish.

Prepare the third marinade.

05

Finishing
To serve, season the plate of fluke slivers with salt, pepper, and Espelette. Add 16 slivers to each of the marinades.

06

Divide the ceviche in the first marinade into three small bowls. Repeat with the fluke in the other two marinades. Sprinkle a small amount of Espelette on the ceviche in each bowl.

Arrange the ceviche in order from simple to complicated, from first marinade to third. Serve immediately.

HALIBUT CASSEROLE

This dish is a simple one, in that it is all cooked in one pot. The sauce is created by simmering everything together, thereby marrying all the ingredients.

RECITE

SERVES 4 – Preparation time: 20 minutes – Cooking time: 15 minutes

- ☐ 1 slice bacon, cut crosswise ¼ inch (6 mm) thick
- ☐ 1 tablespoon butter
- ☐ 8 pearl onions, peeled
- ☐ 12 medium stalks asparagus, peeled and cut into 1 ½ in (38 mm) lengths

- ☐ 2 tablespoons canola oil
- ☐ 4 ounces (115 g) porcini mushrooms
- ☐ 4 ounces (115 g) chanterelle mushrooms
- ☐ 4 ounces (115 g) oyster mushrooms

- ☐ 4 ounces (115 g) morel mushrooms
- ☐ 1 tablespoon chives
- ☐ 2 tablespoons garlic butter (see p. 98)
- ☐ Fine sea salt and freshly ground white pepper

- ☐ 2 cups (480 ml) veal jus (see p. 99)
- ☐ 4 (6-ounce/170 g) halibut fillets
- ☐ 8 pieces tomato confit (see p. 72)

In a small sauté pan, cook the bacon over medium heat until it has rendered its fat and is crisp. Remove the bacon with a slotted spoon and drain on a paper towel. Reserve.

01

In a small sauce pan, melt the butter. Add the pearl onions and 1 tablespoon water. Cook until tender, about 5 minutes.

02

Blanch the asparagus tips in boiling salted water for 1 minute, so that they still have a little bite.

In a large heavy-bottomed casserole, heat the canola oil over medium heat. Add the mushrooms, chives, and garlic butter. Season with salt and pepper and cook until softened, about 5 minutes.

Add veal the jus, and bring to a boil. Add the seasoned halibut. Cover the casserole and cook for 2 minutes. Carefully arrange the pearl onions, asparagus, and bacon around the fish.

05

Bring back to a simmer and cook for another 2 to 3 minutes, until a metal skewer can be easily inserted into the fish and, after left in for 5 seconds, feels just warm when touched to the lip.

06

At this point the fish should be slightly undercooked, as it will continue to cook from residual heat, and be medium-rare once plated.

To serve: Place each fillet in the center of a bowl. Carefully spoon some of the mushrooms and tomatoes evenly around the fish.

Top the fish with chives, pour the sauce around the fish, and serve immediately.

HALIBUT
CITRUS
EMULSION

The simplicity of these ingredients creates surprisingly complex flavors. The combination of the olive oil, citrus juice, and red miso makes a rich yet acidic sauce that compliments the halibut.

RECEIPT

POTATO-FENNEL PURÉE

- ❐ 1 pound (455 g) Yukon gold potatoes
- ❐ 2 tablespoons Milk
- ❐ 8 ounces (225 g) unsalted butter, cubed and chilled
- ❐ 1 bulb fennel, juiced and strained
- ❐ Fine sea salt

CHERRY TOMATO CONFIT

- ❐ 20 cherry tomatoes
- ❐ Fine sea salt
- ❐ Finely ground white pepper
- ❐ 1 cup (240 ml) extra-virgin olive oil
- ❐ 1 sprig rosemary
- ❐ 1 small shallot, peeled and thinly sliced

RED MISO CITRUS EMULSION

- ❐ 2 cups (480 ml) freshly squeezed orange juice

- ❐ 1 teaspoon brunoised ginger
- ❐ ½ shallot, peeled and brunoised
- ❐ 1 teaspoon red miso
- ❐ 1 teaspoon yuzu juice
- ❐ ½ lemon, juiced
- ❐ ½ lime, juiced
- ❐ 3 tablespoons extra-virgin olive oil
- ❐ 1 pinch Espelette pepper

HALIBUT

- ❐ 5½ ounces (155g) portions halibut
- ❐ Fine sea salt
- ❐ Finely ground white pepper
- ❐ ½ gallon poaching liquid (see p. 99)

FINISHING

- ❐ 3 pieces baby fennel, shaved thin on a mandoline
- ❐ 12 pieces micro opal basil

26

Potato-fennel purée

In a pot of salted water, bring the potatoes to a boil, then reduce to a simmer, and cook util tender, about 30 minutes. Drain the potatoes and set aside to let cool slightly. Meanwhile, bring the milk to a boil in a saucepan; remove from heat, cover, and set aside.

01

Peel the potatoes and pass them through a food mill into a saucepan set over low heat. Working in batches, vigorously stir in the butter until the mixture is creamy. Whisk in the warmed milk and fennel juice, season with salt, and set aside.

02

Cherry tomato confit

Preheat the oven to 250°F (120°C). Blanch the tomatoes in boiling water for 5 seconds, then shock them in ice water immediately.

Peel the tomatoes, and put them into a small saucepan. Season lightly with salt and pepper, and add the olive oil, rosemary, and shallot. Cook in the oven for about 40 minutes, until they are tender. Remove the rosemary and shallot, and discard. Set the tomatoes aside.

The tomato confit can be prepared a day in advance and kept in the refrigerator until ready to use.

Red miso citrus emulsion

In a small saucepan, add the orange juice, ginger, shallot, and red miso. Whisk together and cook over medium heat until reduced by half.

05

Add the yuzu juice, lemon juice, and lime juice. While whisking, slowly drizzle in the olive oil. Finish with the Espelette pepper.

06

Halibut

Season the halibut on both sides with salt and pepper and place it in the hot poaching liquid. Poach the fish until a metal skewer inserted into the fish for 5 seconds is met with medium resistance and feels warm when touched to your lip. After removing the halibut from the poaching liquid, season again if needed.

Finishing

Lay out two entrée plates for assembling the dish. Spin a circle of potato purée in the center of the plate. Lay the halibut on top of the potato purée. Garnish with the tomato confit, shaved fennel, and opal basil. Sauce the plate right before serving.

POUNDED TUNA

The only signature dish on the menu at Le Bernardin, this carpaccio represents our style and philosophy. The tuna is the star of the dish, while the foie gras brings elegance and richness, and the thinly sliced baguette gives texture. The addition of the chives, shallots, olive oil, and lemon creates a perfect contrast.

RECIPE

SᴇʀᴠᴇS 4 – Preparation time: starts 2 days before,
20 minutes for the rest of the recipe

FOIE GRAS TERRINE

- ☐ 1 lobe foie gras, about 1½ pounds (680 g)
- ☐ 1 tablespoon fine sea salt
- ☐ ½ teaspoon freshly ground white pepper
- ☐ ¼ teaspoon pinches sel rose
- ☐ 6 cups (1.4 L) chicken stock (see p. 98)

POUNDED TUNA

- ☐ 12 ounces (340 g) sushi-quality yellowfin tuna fillet
- ☐ Marquise-shaped 4 ½-by-9-inch (11-by-23-cm) template

FINISHING

- ☐ 1 mini baguette
- ☐ Fine sea salt
- ☐ Freshly ground white pepper
- ☐ 4 tablespoons (60 ml) extra-virgin olive oil
- ☐ 2 teaspoons peeled and minced shallots
- ☐ 2 tablespoons thinly sliced chives
- ☐ 1 lemon, cut in half

34

Foie gras terrine

Start the preparation 2 days before. Place the lobe of foie gras in ice water overnight. Remove from the water and pat dry. Cover with plastic wrap and let stand at room temperature for 1 hour. Separate the foie gras into two lobes, keeping one covered with a cheesecloth while you work on the other.

01

Starting at the primary vein on the underside of the foie gras, carefully slice through the lobe to the main vein.

02

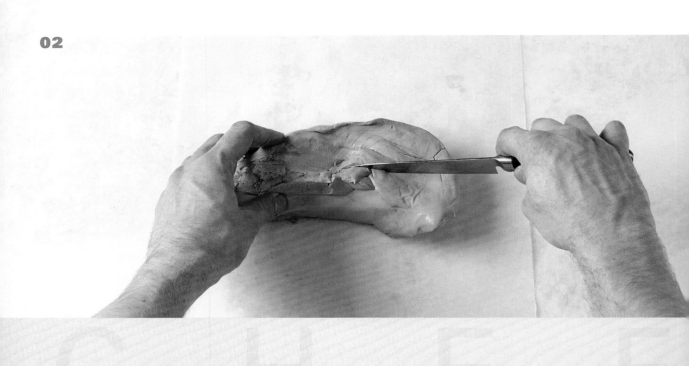

Split the foie gras apart and butterfly the lobe by making an outward cut at each side of the vein.

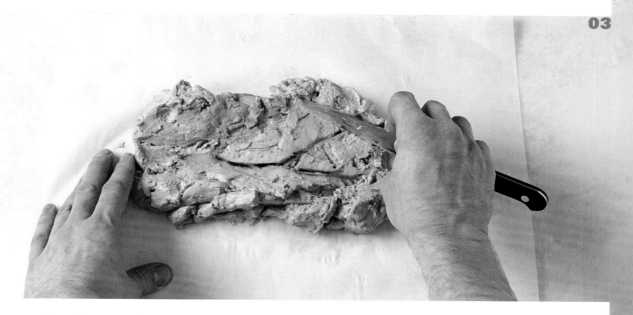

Remove the primary vein and then the small veins throughout the foie gras. Repeat with the remaining lobe.

Mix the salt, pepper, and sel rose together. Season the liver evenly on both sides. Cover the foie gras with plastic wrap and refrigerate for 24 hours.

05

Form the foie gras into a log, approximately 2 ½-inch (6-cm) wide by 6-inches (15-cm) long, on a piece of parchment paper, twisting and squeezing the ends so it is compact.

06

Unwrap the foie gras and transfer on to a piece of cheesecloth. Rolling away from you, roll the foie gras into a tight log, again twisting the ends to compress the shape. Tie one end with a piece of kitchen twine and then the other end.

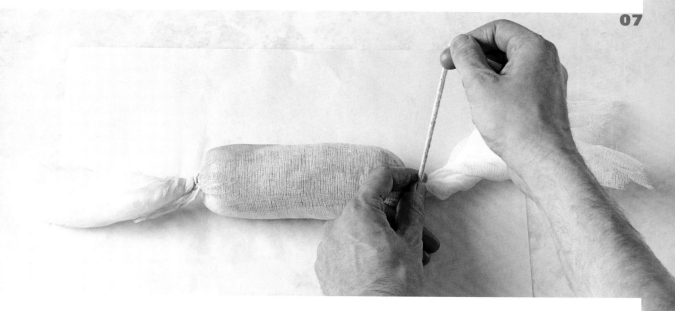

Meanwhile, bring the chicken stock to a boil in a pot large enough to hold the foie gras. Add the foie gras to the stock and cook for 2 minutes, or until it reaches an internal temperature of 90°F (32°C). Remove the foie gras from the stock and chill immediately.

Remove the cheesecloth and reshape the log one more time with plastic wrap. Refrigerate overnight or for up to 12 hours.

09

Pounded tuna
Slice the tuna into ¼-inch (6-mm) thick slices. Lay a large sheet of plastic wrap on a work surface, at least 2 by 3 feet (61 by 91.5 cm).

10

Arrange the tuna pieces, with an inch between slices, on the plastic. Cover the tuna with another large sheet of plastic.

Using a kitchen mallet, gently pound the tuna into a very thin and even layer of tuna about ⅛-inch (3-mm) thick.

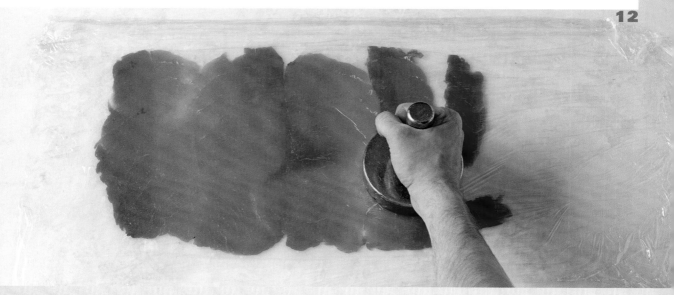

To help get the tuna to an even thickness, add a few drops of oil on the top layer of plastic and gently slide the mallet from side to side on top of the plastic. This will help to smooth out any bumps and make all the portions the same thickness.

Using the template and a sharp knife, cut through the tuna and both layers of plastic to get four marquise-shaped portions. Refrigerate the tuna for at least 30 minutes; it can be pounded and cut a few hours ahead of time.

13

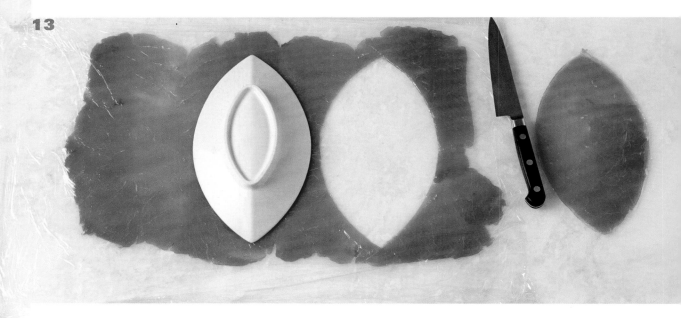

Finishing

Preheat the oven to 350°F (175°C). Slice the bread into 4 very thin slices, lengthwise. Arrange the slices on a parchment paper lined baking sheet; cover with parchment paper and another baking sheet so the slices stay as flat as possible. Toast the slices in the oven until they are lightly browned and crisp, 5 to 7 minutes. Allow the slices to cool to room temperature.

14

To serve, slice four thin pieces (about ⅛-inch [3-mm thick]) of foie gras, making sure each slice is as long as the baguette slices. Place the foie gras slices on top of the baguette slices. Place each baguette in the center of an oval plate. Pull the top piece of plastic wrap off of a portion of tuna. Invert the tuna (so the remaining plastic-wrapped side is in your hand) and place it on top of the foie gras baguette. Pull the other piece of plastic wrap off the tuna.

Season the tuna with salt and pepper and brush with olive oil. Sprinkle shallots and chives over piece of tuna. Wipe off the excess garnish. Squeeze lemon juice over each portion and serve immediately.

RED SNAPPER

AND CEPES
IN PORT REDUCTION

The ingredients in this dish are quite simple;
it's the technique for preparing the sauce that
is key. That's what gives this dish its wonderful
consistency and shines.

RECITE

- ❏ 2 cups (480 ml) 10-year-old excellent-quality port
- ❏ 2 cups (480 ml) good-quality sherry vinegar
- ❏ 3 tablespoons corn oil

- ❏ 1 pound (455 g) fresh or frozen cepes, stems cut lengthwise into slices ¼ inch (6 mm) wide, caps halved if small or cut into 3 or 4 slices if large
- ❏ 2 sprigs fresh thyme

- ❏ 1 clove garlic, peeled and halved
- ❏ 1 large shallot, peeled and finely diced
- ❏ Fine sea salt, to taste
- ❏ Freshly ground white pepper, to taste

- ❏ 5 tablespoons (70 g) unsalted butter
- ❏ 4 (6-ounce/170-g) red snapper fillets
- ❏ ¼ teaspoon Chinese five-spice powder
- ❏ 4 teaspoons minced fresh chives

46

Bring the port to a boil in a medium-size heavy saucepan over medium-high heat. Lower the heat slightly and simmer until reduced to 1 cup (240 ml) (if using a gas stove, never let the flames extend above the bottom edge of the pan). Add the vinegar and simmer until reduced almost to a syrup consistency, lowering the heat as necessary and watching carefully to keep it from burning around the edges—you should have about 7 tablespoons (100 ml).

01

Divide 1 tablespoon of corn oil between two skillets and place them over high heat until just smoking. Divide the cepes, thyme, and garlic between the skillets and lower the heat to medium. Sauté until browned, about 4 minutes.

02

Turn the heat to low and divide the shallot, salt, pepper, and 2 tablespoons of butter between the skillets. Cook until the shallot is softened and the cepes are tender, about 6 minutes. Discard the garlic and thyme and combine the two mixtures.

Season the snapper on both sides with salt and pepper. Sprinkle the five-spice powder over the skin and rub it in.

Clean the skillets and divide the remaining 2 tablespoons of corn oil between them. Place both over high heat until just smoking. Add the snapper to the skillets, skin side down, and briefly hold the fillets down with a spatula to prevent the skin from shrinking.

Sauté until the bottom is dark and crusted, about 5 minutes. Turn and cook until a metal skewer inserted into the fish for 5 seconds is met with medium resistance and feels warm when touched to your lip, about 5 minutes longer. Keep warm.

Meanwhile, reheat the mushrooms. Bring the sauce to a boil over high heat. Cut the remaining 3 tablespoons of butter into ½-inch (12-mm) pieces. Lift the saucepan a few inches above the heat and add the butter. Shake the pan back and forth until the butter is melted and incorporated into the sauce; this will take about 3 minutes.

Do not stir or whisk the butter into the sauce. When ready, the sauce will be very shiny and clear.

To serve, stir the chives into the mushrooms and arrange them in the center of four large plates. Top with the snapper. Drizzle the sauce around the mushrooms and serve immediately.

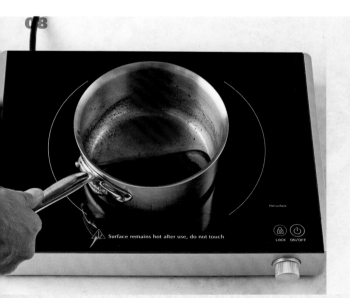

08

SALMON
RED WINE
BÉARNAISE

While this dish is called a red wine béarnaise,
it is more like a *beurre rouge*, but with all
the aromatics of a traditional béarnaise, and
much lighter.

SERVES 4 – Preparation time: 20 minutes – Cooking time: 15 minutes

RED WINE BÉARNAISE

- ☐ ½ cup (120 ml) red wine
- ☐ ½ cup (120 ml) red wine vinegar
- ☐ 1 tablespoon black peppercorns
- ☐ 1 teaspoon minced shallot
- ☐ 3 sprigs tarragon
- ☐ 1 sprig thyme

- ☐ 3 tablespoons (45 ml) brown butter sauce (see p. 98)
- ☐ 4 tablespoons (55 g) unsalted butter
- ☐ Salt
- ☐ Pepper

POTATO CRISPS

- ☐ 1 Yukon gold potato

- ☐ 2 cups (480 g) canola oil
- ☐ Fine sea salt
- ☐ Freshly ground white pepper

SALMON

- ☐ Fine sea salt
- ☐ 4 (6-ounce/170-g) salmon fillets, skin off
- ☐ Freshly ground white pepper

FINISHING

- ☐ ½ teaspoon thinly sliced fresh tarragon
- ☐ ½ tablespoon minced shallots
- ☐ 1 teaspoon coarsely ground black pepper
- ☐ 4 to 5 sea bean sprouts, broken into 2-inch (5-cm) pieces

Red wine béarnaise

Combine the wine, vinegar, peppercorns, shallot, tarragon, and thyme. Bring to a boil and reduce to 2 tablespoons. Add the brown butter sauce and then gradually whisk in the whole butter.

Strain through a fine-mesh sieve and transfer to a small pot. Season with salt and pepper. Keep warm.

Potato crisps

Slice the potato into very thin slices. Using a cookie cutter, cut 1-inch (2.5-cm) round circles from the slices (you will need 20 slices total).

Heat the canola oil in a small deep pot to 300°F (150°C). Fry the potato circles in the hot oil until they are golden brown and crisp. Drain on to a paper towel–lined plate and season with salt and white pepper.

Salmon

Put about ½ cup (120 ml) of water in a pan (just enough to cover the surface), season with salt, and bring to a simmer over medium heat. Season the salmon on both sides with salt and white pepper. Place the salmon in the pan; cook at barely a simmer until the top of the fish is just warm to the touch, about 3 minutes.

05

Finishing

While the salmon is cooking, to create a garnish here mix together the tarragon, shallots, and black pepper in a small bowl and gently warm the red wine béarnaise.

06

Be sure to cook the salmon very slowly, so that it cooks evenly. If cooked too quickly, the salmon will release fat and protein and become hard and dry.

To plate, remove the salmon from the pot and drain each fillet on a towel. Plate each fillet in the center of the plate.

Sprinkle a little of the garnish down the center of the salmon and place potato crisps and bean on top. Pour the warm red wine béarnaise around the plate.

SEA
MEDLEY

Inspired by a traditional *chawanmushi* (Japanese egg custard), the flan, together with the broth, heightens the flavors of the shellfish.

RECODE

SERVES 4 – Preparation time: 25 minutes – Cooking time: 20 minutes

SHRIMP

- ☐ ¼ pound (115 g) 36-40 shrimp, peeled, cleaned and deveined
- ☐ Fine sea salt
- ☐ Freshly around white pepper
- ☐ 2 tablespoons butter, melted

SEA URCHIN CUSTARD

- ☐ 1 cup sea urchin roe (about 8 ounces/225 g)
- ☐ ½ cup (120 ml) heavy cream
- ☐ ½ cup (120 ml) milk
- ☐ 1 egg yolk
- ☐ Fine sea salt
- ☐ Freshly ground white pepper
- ☐ Espelette pepper

DASHI

- ☐ 2 cups (480 ml) water
- ☐ ½ ounce kombu
- ☐ 1 ½ ounce (6 to 8 flakes) *kezurikatsuo* (larger, thicker shavings of dried bonito)
- ☐ ½ ounce shaved (thin) bonito flakes
- ☐ 2 teaspoons soy sauce

FINISHING

- ☐ ¼ pound (115 g) peekytoe crab meat
- ☐ Fine sea salt
- ☐ Freshly ground white pepper
- ☐ 2 tablespoons butter, melted
- ☐ 12 large tongues of sea urchin roe
- ☐ 1 piece fresh yuzu

Shrimp

Preheat the oven to 350°F (175°C). Place the peeled shrimp in an ovenproof pan and season with salt and white pepper. Brush each shrimp with melted butter, place the pan in the oven and bake for 4 to 6 minutes, until the shrimp just turn opaque. Let cool, and cut in half lengthwise. Set aside.

01

Sea urchin custard

Purée the sea urchin roe in a blender. Add the heavy cream, milk, and egg yolk; season with salt, white pepper, and Espelette.

02

Strain through a fine-mesh sieve and pour the custard base into four small soup bowls, or four cleaned sea urchin shells.

Place the custards in a baking pan filled with about 1-inch (2.5-cm) of water. Cover the baking pan with aluminum foil. Place in the oven and bake the custards until they are set in the middle, 8 to 12 minutes. Remove from the oven, and set aside in a warm place.

The custards are best cooked in a convection oven. If you have a conventional oven, the cooking time might be slightly longer and the pan should be rotated halfway through cooking.

Dashi
Bring the water and the kombu to a boil. Simmer the kombu for 2 minutes.

05

Remove the pot from the stove, add the *kezurikatsûo* and allow it to steep for 3 minutes.

06

Add the bonito flakes and let them steep for 10 minutes.

Strain the dashi through a fine-mesh sieve. Add the soy sauce and set aside.

Finishing

Lay out the crab and shrimp on a small sheet pan and lightly season with salt and Espelette. Drizzle with melted butter and warm in the oven.

09

Reheat the custards in the oven and bring the dashi up to a boil. Remove the crab, shrimp, and custards from the oven once they are warm.

To assemble, lay the crab and shrimp gently on top of each custard.

Place the tongues of sea urchin roe in with the crab and shrimp, on top of the custards. Grate fresh yuzu on top. Serve the dashi on the side, or pour it on top of the custard right before serving.

SHRIMP, TOMATO, AND BASIL "PIZZA"

This dish is very similar to a real pizza, but the texture of the phylo crust makes it more refined.

RECITE

TOMATO CONFIT

- ❏ 2¼ pounds (1.1 kg) ripe tomatoes (about 7 medium)
- ❏ 2 tablespoons extra-virgin olive oil
- ❏ 3 cloves garlic, peeled and finely chopped
- ❏ 2 large shallots, peeled and finely chopped

- ❏ 1 sprig fresh thyme
- ❏ ¼ teaspoon chopped fresh rosemary
- ❏ 1 teaspoon fine sea salt
- ❏ ¼ teaspoon freshly ground white pepper

PASTRY

- ❏ 5 sheets frozen phyllo dough, defrosted

- ❏ ⅓ cup (75 g) unsalted butter, melted

SHRIMP

- ❏ 1 tablespoon unsalted butter, melted
- ❏ 54 uncooked medium shrimp (about 3 pounds/ 1.4 kg) peeled, deveined, and sliced in half horizontally

- ❏ Fine sea salt
- ❏ Freshly ground white pepper, to taste
- ❏ Cayenne pepper, to taste
- ❏ 36 long saffron threads
- ❏ ¾ teaspoon fresh thyme leaves
- ❏ 3 tablespoons extra-virgin olive oil
- ❏ 6 fresh basil leaves, cut into thin strips

Tomato confit

Blanch the tomatoes in boiling water for 5 seconds, then dip ice water until cold.

Peel, cut in half crosswise, and squeeze out the seeds. Finely chop the tomatoes and set aside.

Heat the olive oil in a large saucepan over medium-high heat. Add the garlic and shallots, lower the heat slightly, and sauté until softened, about 3 minutes. Add the thyme and rosemary. Stir in the tomatoes, tomato paste, salt, and pepper. Lower the heat to medium and simmer, stirring occasionally, for 12 minutes.

Take out the thyme and simmer until the mixture is thick, about 8 minutes longer.

Pastry

Preheat the oven to 375°F (190°C). Lay 1 sheet of phyllo dough on a work surface, keeping the rest covered with a damp cloth until needed. Brush with melted butter and top with another sheet of phyllo. Repeat until all of the phyllo and butter are used.

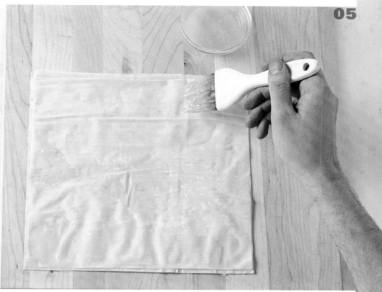

05

Using a ring as a guide, cut out 6 circles of phyllo, discarding the scraps. Line a large baking sheet with parchment paper and put the phyllo circles on the pan (bake in two batches if necessary to fit).

Cover with another sheet of parchment, pressing the paper into the phyllo. Bake until the pastry is well browned, about 12 minutes. Set aside.

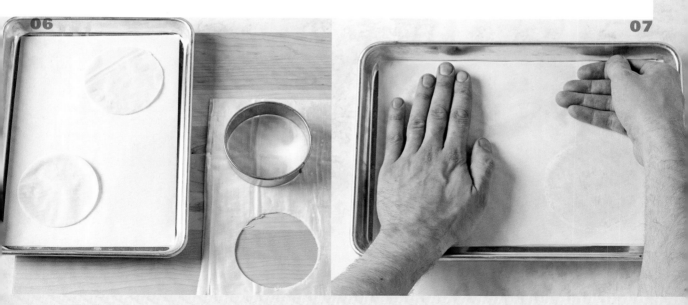

06

07

Shrimp

Using the ring as a guide, cut 12 circles of parchment paper. Brush 6 of these with butter. Put the ring over one of the buttered rounds as a guide to keep the shrimp in an even circle. Arrange the shrimp halves in a radial pattern on top of the parchment, cut side down, as close together as possible so they completely cover the paper. Repeat with the remaining shrimp, covering the 6 buttered papers. Press the unbuttered parchment rounds over the shrimp. Place the shrimp rounds on a baking sheet and refrigerate until ready to use.

Preheat the oven to 550°F (290°C). Work quickly from this point or the pastry will get soggy. Spread the tomato confit on the phyllo rounds. Pull the top sheet of parchment off the shrimp. Season with salt and pepper. Invert the shrimp rounds over the phyllo, so the edges line up perfectly. Pull off the parchment.

10

Be sure not to over-cook the shrimp as they will curl up on the pizza.

Season the top of the shrimp with salt and pepper and sprinkle very lightly with cayenne. Scatter the saffron and thyme over the shrimp and drizzle each pizza with 1 teaspoon of olive oil.

Put on a baking sheet (or divide between two) and bake until the shrimp turns pink, about 5 minutes. Scatter the basil over the pizzas and drizzle another ½ teaspoon of oil over each one. Place on plates and serve immediately.

SMOKED SALMON CROQUE MONSIEUR WITH CAVIAR

For this croque monsieur, smoked salmon is used instead of ham, and it is seasoned with lemon zest and chives. The cheese is Gruyère and the bread is buttered and grilled in a pan, though it could be pressed in a traditional croque monsieur mold and held over the flame the way my grandmother did.

RECIPE

SERVES 4 – Preparation time: 15 minutes – Cooking Time: 5 minutes

- ❏ 4 ounces (115 g) Gruyère cheese
- ❏ 8 slices Pullman bread (or good-quality white bread), ½-inch (12-mm) thick
- ❏ 8 ounces (225 g) sliced smoked salmon
- ❏ 1 tablespoon lemon confit, cut into tiny dice (see p. 98)
- ❏ 1 tablespoon sliced chives
- ❏ 1 ounce (30 g) Osetra caviar
- ❏ 6 tablespoons (85 g) unsalted butter, softened

Using a Japanese mandoline, or a vegetable peeler, slice the Gruyère very thin.

01

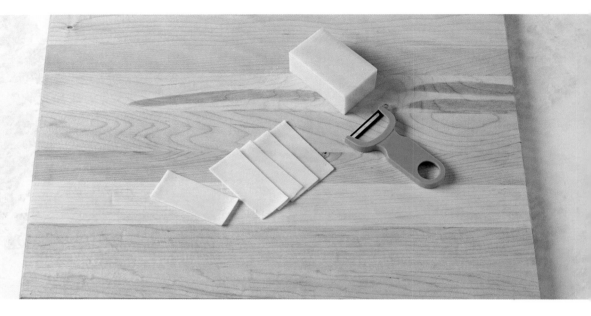

Place the bread slices out on a table. On 4 slices, place the Gruyère and on the other 4 slices, place the smoked salmon. Sprinkle the salmon slices with the lemon confit and chives. Close the sandwiches.

02

Using a serrated knife, cut off the crusts.

Before serving, separate the bread from the salmon side of the sandwiches, and spread ¼ ounce of caviar evenly on each sandwich. Put the sandwiches back together.

Spread the softened butter on the outsides of the sandwiches.

05

Preheat a nonstick sauté pan over medium-high heat. Add the sandwiches to the pan with the Gruyère side down and sauté for 2 minutes.

06

The butter should be spread on the bread, not put into the pan. This will ensure that you get even browning on both sides and that the butter doesn't burn when the sandwich is flipped. The sandwich should be cooked until the cheese is just starting to melt, but the salmon is still raw. If the salmon is cooked, it will become dry and salty.

Turn the sandwiches over and sauté for 1 minute on the salmon side.

To serve, slice the croque monsieurs on the diagonal, then on the diagonal again (you will have four triangles). Arrange the triangles on a plate. Serve immediately.

LOBSTER
CAPUCCINO

The earthiness of the celery root complements the sweetness
of the lobster. The black truffle and the lobster coral foam are
a nice finish to this luxurious dish.

RECIPE

SERVES 4 – Preparation Time: 45 minutes – Cooking Time: 5 minutes

CELERIAC SOUP

- ❏ 2 cups (300 g) celeriac, cut into 1-inch (2.5-cm) dice
- ❏ 2 tablespoons unsalted butter

- ❏ Fine sea salt
- ❏ Freshly ground pepper

LOBSTER FOAM

- ❏ 12 ounces (340 g) lobster boddies

- ❏ 1 tablespoon tomato paste
- ❏ 1 cup (240 ml) heavy brandy
- ❏ 8 ounces cream
- ❏ 1 tablespoon lobster roe

FINISHING

- ❏ 4 ounces (115 g) lobster, diced
- ❏ 1 teaspoon unsalted butter
- ❏ ½ ounce (15 g) truffles, grated

Celeriac soup

Place the celeriac in a pot with 1 ½ cups (360 ml) water and the butter. Season with sea salt and freshly ground pepper. Simmer until tender.

01

Place the celeriac in a blender and purée until smooth, using the cooking liquid as needed to thin. Reserve.

02

Lobster foam

Heat a rondeau over medium-high heat and sear the lobster bodies for 2 minutes, or until they turn bright red. Add the tomato paste and cook for 2 minutes. Add the brandy and reduce slightly. Add the cream and simmer for 15 minutes.

Remove from the heat and strain through a fine-mesh sieve. Using a handheld immersion blender, temper in the lobster roe. Reserve.

When adding the lobster roe, the sauce should be kept hot but not boiling. This should be whisked continually on low heat until the sauce is bright red. If the lobster foam is not cooked enough, the sauce will have a greenish-gray tinge to it.

Finishing

To serve, warm the diced lobster in the butter and 1 tablespoon water. Season with sea salt and freshly ground pepper.

05

Bring the soup to a boil, thinning with water if necessary. Bring the lobster cream to a boil; remove from the heat and, using a handheld immersion blender, mix until very frothy.

06

Divide the lobster meat between four bowls and pour the soup over the lobster.

Spoon the lobster foam over the soup and sprinkle the truffle over the foam. Serve immediately.

GLOSSARY

GLOS SARY

BLANCH
To cook an ingredient in boiling water for a short period of time and then plunge into an ice-water bath to stop the cooking process.

BRUNOISE
A basic knife cut measuring $\frac{1}{8}$ by $\frac{1}{8}$ by $\frac{1}{8}$.

CANOLA OIL
A vegetable oil made from rapeseed.

JULIENNE
To cut ingredients into long, thin, match-like strips.

KEZURIKATSUO
Thick shavings of dried skipjack tuna.

KOMBU
Edible kelp (seaweed), commonly used in making dashis and broths.

PEEKYTOE CRAB
Otherwise known as Atlantic Rock Crab.

PONZU
A citrus-and-soy-based sauce commonly used in Japanese cuisine.

RED MISO
A traditional Japanese paste made from fermented soybeans and sometimes rice and barley.

YUKON GOLD POTATO
A yellow-fleshed variety of potato.

BASIC RECIPES

BROWN BUTTER SAUCE

Makes 1 cup
- ½ pound unsalted butter
- 1 cup reduced chicken stock (see below)
- 1 tablespoon lemon juice
- Fine sea salt and freshly ground white pepper, to taste

Brown the butter in a pot over medium-high heat, whisking occasionally. Set aside.
Warm the chicken stock and combine it with the lemon juice.
Using an immersion blender, slowly add the brown butter to the chicken stock and lemon juice. Season to taste with sea salt and white pepper.

CHICKEN STOCK

Makes 3 quarts
- 6 pounds chicken backs
- 5 quarts cold water

Rinse the chicken well under cold running water and place it in a medium-size stockpot. Cover with water; the chicken should be covered by 2 inches.

Bring the water to a boil and then turn the heat down to a low simmer. Simmer the stock for 3 hours, carefully skimming away with a ladle any fat and impurities that rise to the surface. Discard the fat and impurities.
Remove the stock from the heat and strain it through a fine-mesh sieve, being careful not to press too much of the chicken and sediment into and through the sieve. Degrease the stock again with a ladle.
Quickly cool the stock and store, refrigerated, until ready to use. Scrape off any remaining fat before using.

GARLIC BUTTER

Makes 1 pound
- 2 tablespoons chopped fresh Italian parsley
- 1 pound unsalted butter, at room temperature
- ¼ cup, peeled and minced garlic
- 2 tablespoons, peeled and minced shallot

Place the parsley in a cheesecloth and squeeze to remove excess moisture. Place the butter in a mixer and whip until it is creamy. Add the garlic, shallot, and parsley to the butter and mix well.
Transfer the butter to a tightly sealed plastic container. Store, refrigerated, until ready to use.

LEMON CONFIT

Makes 24
- 5 cups kosher salt
- 5 tablespoons sugar
- 6 lemons

Combine the salt and sugar and mix well.
Trim the end off each lemon. Quarter each lemon lengthwise. Toss the lemons with half of the salt/sugar mix, coating each lemon.
Pour a layer of the salt/sugar mix into the bottom of a plastic container. Layer the lemons into the container, being sure to pack additional salt/sugar mix between and around the lemons. Pour a generous amount of the salt/sugar mix on top of the last layer of lemons.
Tightly seal the container with a lid. Refrigerate for at least 2 weeks before using, though the lemons are best after 3 months and will keep for up to a year (keep them in the salt/sugar mix until ready to use).
To use, thoroughly rinse the lemons with water. Cut away all of the flesh from the rinds of the lemons; discard the flesh. Mince or julienne the rinds as needed. Lightly blanch the rinds (before cutting) if using as a garnish that will not be cooked.

POACHING LIQUID

Makes 2 gallons
- [ ] 8 ounces unsalted butter
- [ ] 2 cups all-purpose flour
- [ ] 2 gallons water
- [ ] ¾ cup fresh orange juice
- [ ] 1 cup fresh lemon juice
- [ ] 2 tablespoons vermouth
- [ ] Kosher salt, to taste

Prepare a blond roux by melting the butter in a small pot over medium heat. Add the flour and stir until the mixture is smooth. Cook the roux, stirring constantly, until it is a golden straw color and has a slightly nutty aroma. Cool the roux to help prevent lumps when it is added to the hot liquid.

Bring the water to a boil in a medium-size pot.

Add the orange juice, lemon juice, and vermouth to the water and bring to a boil.

Add half of the cold roux to the hot liquid, whisking well.

Add the rest of the roux and bring the liquid to a boil again (it should look like a thick soup). Season with salt and allow the poaching liquid to simmer until all the flour flavor has cooked out (about 15 minutes).

Remove the poaching liquid from the direct heat but keep it warm near the stove until ready to use; whisk the poaching liquid occasionally to prevent a skin from forming.

VEAL STOCK

Makes 4 quarts
- [ ] 15 pounds veal knuckles and bones
- [ ] 10 quarts cold water

Rinse the veal bones well under cold running water and place them in a medium-size stockpot. Add water; there should be twice the amount as water to the amount of bones.

Slowly bring the water to a simmer; carefully skimming away with a ladle any fat and impurities that rise to the surface.

As soon as the liquid comes to a simmer, remove from the heat and drain the bones through a colander.

Rinse the bones well, making sure the water runs clean and all of the impurities are removed.

Return the bones to a clean stockpot. Add 10 quarts of cold water, bring to a boil, and then turn the heat down to a low simmer.

Simmer the stock for 6 hours, skimming frequently with a ladle to remove any fat and impurities.

Remove the stock from the heat and strain it through a fine-mesh sieve. Degrease the stock again with a ladle.

Quickly cool the stock and store, refrigerated until ready to use. Scrape off any remaining fat before using.

VEAL JUS

Makes 2 quarts
- [ ] 2 tablespoons canola oil
- [ ] 10 pounds veal shoulder, cut into 2-inch (5-cm) pieces
- [ ] 1 small carrot, peeled and diced
- [ ] 2 ribs celery, diced
- [ ] 1 medium onion, diced
- [ ] 4 quarts veal stock (see left)

Heat a large stockpot over medium-high heat.

Add the canola oil and then the veal. Sear the veal shoulder for 15 to 20 minutes, until it is golden brown in color, stirring periodically so the meat does not stick to the pot. Add the carrot, celery, and onion and continue to cook over medium heat.

Cover the veal with stock. Bring to a boil, lower the temperature, and simmer the jus for 2 to 2 ½ hours.

Strain the veal jus into a clean stockpot and reduce to 2 quarts.

ADDRESS BOOK
ERIC RIPERT

UNITED
STATES

LE BERNARDIN
155 WEST 51ST STREET
NEW YORK, NY 10019
TEL: +1 212 554 1515
FAX: +1 212 554 1100

BLUE BY ERIC RIPERT
THE RITZ-CARLTON,
GRAND CAYMAN
SEVEN MILE BEACH,
GRAND CAYMAN,
CAYMAN ISLANDS
TEL: +1 345 943-9000

PRODUCT INDEX

PRODUCT INDEX

AKNOWLEDGMENTS

Maguy Le Coze and all the Le Bernardin family. Special thanks to Adam Plitt, Angie Mosier, and Nigel Parry for their passionate contribution to this book.

THE ART OF BOOKS SINCE 1949

115 West 18th Street
New York, NY 10011
www.abramsbooks.com

COLLECTION DIRECTOR
Emmanuel Jirou-Najou

EDITORIAL MANAGER
Alice Gouget

PHOTOGRAPHER & INTERVIEW
Angela Mosier

GRAPHIC DESIGN
Soins graphiques
Thanks to Sophie

PHOTOENGRAVING
Nord Compo

MARKETING & COMMUNICATION MANAGER
Camille Gonnet
camille.gonnet@alain-ducasse.com

ISBN 978-2-84123-726-5
© Alain Ducasse Édition 2014
84, avenue Victor Cresson
92130 Issy-les-Moulineaux
France
http://www.alain-ducasse.com/en/livres-ebooks-applications

The editor thanks Bowery Kitchen, our exclusive supplier for this book.

COOK
WITH YOUR
FAVORITE
CHEFS

PIERRE
HERMÉ
ALAIN DUCASSE
PUBLISHING

ALAIN
DUCASSE
ALAIN DUCASSE
PUBLISHING

DANIEL
BOULUD
ALAIN DUCASSE
PUBLISHING

my **BEST**

ILLUSTRATED **COOKING COURSES** FROM **FINEST CHEFS**
TO HELP YOU PRODUCE THEIR **TOP 10 RECIPES** WITH
PERFECT RESULTS EVERY TIME!

ALAIN DUCASSE
PUBLISHING

www.alain-ducasse.com